Communication policies in **Sri Lanka**

In this series

Communication policies in Ireland
Communication policies in Sweden
Communication policies in Hungary
Communication policies in the Federal Republic of Germany
Communication policies in Brazil
Communication policies in Yugoslavia
Communication policies in Costa Rica
Communication policies in India
Communication policies in Peru
Communication policies in Sri Lanka

Communication policies in **Sri Lanka**

A study carried out by a committee
appointed by the Secretary to the Ministry of Education, Sri Lanka,
and written by M. A. de Silva and Reggie Siriwardene

Published in 1977 by the United Nations Educational, Scientific
and Cultural Organization,
7 Place de Fontenoy, 75700 Paris
Printed by Snoeck-Ducaju & Son, Ghent (Belgium)

ISBN 92-3-101416-1
Les politiques de la communication en Sri Lanka 92-3-201416-5

Preface

Communication policies are sets of principles and norms established to guide the behaviour of communication systems. They are shaped over time in the context of society's general approach to communication and to the media. Emanating from political ideologies, the social and economic conditions of the country and the values on which they are based, they strive to relate these to the real needs for and the prospective opportunities of communication.

Communication policies exist in every society, though they may sometimes be latent and disjointed, rather than clearly articulated and harmonized. They may be very general, in the nature of desirable goals and principles, or they may be more specific and practically binding. They may exist or be formulated at many levels. They may be incorporated in the constitution or legislation of a country; in over-all national policies, in the guidelines for individual administrations, in professional codes of ethics as well as in the constitutions and operational rules of particular communication institutions.

The publication of this series of studies has been undertaken as part of the programme adopted by the General Conference of Unesco at its sixteenth session, related to the analysis of communication policies as they exist at the different levels—public, institutional, professional—in selected countries. The aim of the series is to present this information in a manner which can be comparable. Thus an attempt has been made to follow, as far as possible, a fairly similar structural pattern and method of approach which was agreed between the national institutions undertaking the work.

This survey of communication policy in Sri Lanka has been carried out by M. A. de Silva and Reggie Siriwardene at the request of the Sri Lanka National Commission for Unesco. The opinions expressed by the authors do not necessarily reflect the views of Unesco.

Authors' acknowledgements

We wish to thank Dr Premadasa Udagama, the Secretary to the Ministry of Education, who entrusted us with the task of writing this study, and Mr D. K. Subasinghe, Secretary of the National Commission for Unesco in Sri Lanka, for his untiring efforts in stimulating us to bring it to completion. We are grateful also for the assistance rendered by Mr Malcolm Wijithapala, Assistant Director of Information, as our secretary.

Contents

Contents

Introduction

Sri Lanka (by which ancient and traditional name the country has been known to its own people from time immemorial) was called by the name 'Ceylon' in the English language, and by related names in other European languages. Since 1972, the name 'Sri Lanka' which was adopted as the official name of the country under the new Constitution of the Republic, has come into general international use with reference to the island. We have used the name Sri Lanka throughout this study, irrespective of period, except in names of publications and institutions dating from an earlier era where 'Ceylon' occurred or occurs as a constituent part.

Sri Lanka presents a pattern of social and political evolution that is in many ways unique among the countries of the Third World. Its people have had experience of universal franchise for nearly half a century, and of free universal education for thirty years. With the consequent high rate of literacy, there has grown up a democratic political consciousness which has enabled its people to change governments by peaceful means five times in the last twenty-eight years, that is since independence in 1948. For all these reasons the study of communication and communication policies in Sri Lanka should be of considerable interest to observers and students elsewhere. It is in this hope that the present survey is presented.

1 The idea of communication policy

For a country such as Sri Lanka, which has in recent times achieved independence after a long period of colonial rule, the central task is that of national development. Only through the development of its economy, by the most effective utilization of its natural resources and of the energies of its people, can Sri Lanka achieve prosperity for the nation and lay the foundations for general social, intellectual, cultural and spiritual development.

Sri Lanka is a democracy with one of the longest traditions of parliamentary government among the countries of the Third World. The people have exercised the right of universal franchise since 1931, that is, seventeen years before the attainment of independence. In 1972, a Constituent Assembly, acting on a mandate from the people, adopted a new constitution which affirmed the sovereignty of the people and removed residual limitations on its exercise.

The people of Sri Lanka cherish their sovereignty and are firmly wedded to democratic traditions of government. Economic development in Sri Lanka must therefore take place within a framework of democracy, which means that the people are always the final arbiters of policies and programmes of development.

But the democratic basis of development does not mean only that the people are called upon once in several years to choose between contending programmes and to elect a government to execute the policy they choose. In a democracy there can be no effective economic development without the willing and enthusiastic participation of the people in the process of development. Living democracy involves the continuous day-to-day participation of the people in the process of decision-making and the execution of policies.

It is in this context that communication and communication policy assume great importance for a developing country such as Sri Lanka. Communication is the essential means by which people are drawn into conscious and active participation in the process of development on a democratic basis. Fundamentally, therefore, communication policy, as worked out and effected by governments and public institutions, mass-media organizations, and the entire range of people involved in the process of communication, must be judged by their success or failure in achieving this objective of popular participation.

Recent sociological thinking about mass communication has drawn attention to the deficiencies of older models of communication which conceived of it as a one-way transmission of information from source to receiver. Even when this model is modified by providing for the possibilities of what is technically called 'feedback', it still remains fundamentally a conception of a one-way process in which the source of communication decides the content of what is communicated, with perhaps minor modifications as a result of reactions from the receiver.

In contrast, writers such as L. S. Harms and J. Richstad have proposed an interchange model of human communication, in which the distinction between source and receiver ceases to be useful or even possible. Communication in this sense is seen as a genuine dialogue, in which there is continuous interaction between all those who participate in the activity of communication.

The importance of these different conceptions of human communication for the present purpose is that the one-way model of communication is oligarchic, elitist or authoritarian, whereas the interchange model of communication is participatory and therefore truly democratic. But the former model can apply in practice in a society where the external forms of democracy exist but communication is regarded as a means of manipulating people and influencing or inducing them to think and act in ways that have been decided by those who control the means of communication.

All interpersonal communication in daily life among people who meet each other in relations of friendliness, intimacy and equality, is participatory. But in a modern society one of the most vital and difficult tasks is that of preserving this participatory character of communication in the complex relationships of power, administration and economic management in contemporary life. In particular, modern mass media are based on the distance between source and receiver and on the differentiation between the active communicator who commands the technical means of communication and the passive receiver who reads, listens or sees and, therefore, they lend themselves very easily to the manipulation of people by those who control the media. It is the task of a democratic society to find the means of combating these tendencies of the mass media as well as to find other modes of preserving the participatory character of communication that is vital for development.

This publication will examine communication and communication policy in Sri Lanka from the standpoint outlined above. While describing and assessing the functioning of the mass media in this country, it will seek to show that Sri Lanka has possessed a long tradition of oral and interpersonal modes of communication, which are still active and often play a more decisive role in determining the direction of society than the mass media.

Since Sri Lanka has gone through rapid social and political change in recent times, this study will give special attention to the historical evolution of modes of communication and the social context in which such evolution took place, since the problems of the present and the direction of the future often cannot be understood except in relation to the inheritance of the past.

2 The tradition of oral and interpersonal communication

In traditional society in Sri Lanka the skills of reading and writing were confined to a minority consisting of monks, courtiers, nobles and professional persons, but there was a richly developed oral culture which embraced the whole community. One of the most perceptive observers of the old Kandyan (hill-country) Kingdom, was Robert Knox, a sailor in the service of the British East India Company, who was a prisoner for nearly twenty years in Sri Lanka during the seventeenth century. In his book *An Historical Relation of Ceylon* (1681), Knox testifies to the paucity of the skills of literacy on the one hand and to the richness of the oral culture among the people of the Kandyan Kingdom. He writes:[1]

Their Learning is but small. All they ordinarily learn is to read and to write. But it is no shame to a man if he can do neither.

On the other hand, he writes:[2]

Their language is Copious, Smooth Elegant, Courtly; according as the People that speak it are. Who are full of words, Titles and Complements. . . . Their ordinary Plow-men and Husbandmen do speak elegantly, and are full of complement. And there is no difference between the ability and speech of a Country-man and a Courtier. When any hath a favour to beg of a Nobleman, or any business with him, they do not abruptly speak their desires or errand at first, but bring it in with a long harangue of his worth or good disposition or abilities; and this in very handsome and taking stile. They bring up their Children to speak after this manner, and use them to go with errands to great men; and they are able to tell their tale very well also.

Knox's account leaves us in no doubt that in traditional society in Sri Lanka civilized personal intercourse through speech and conversation was a highly developed art. But his book also throws light on the modes of communication through which knowledge of public affairs was diffused throughout the community.[3]

At their leisure when their affairs will permit, they commonly meet at places built for strangers and way-faring men to lodge in, in their language called Amblomb,

1. Robert Knox, *An Historical Relation of Ceylon,* Part III, Chapter 10, 1681.
2. ibid., Chapter 9.
3. ibid., Chapter 8.

where they sit chewing Betel, and looking one upon the other very gravely and solidly, discoursing concerning the affairs at Court, between the King and the great Men; and what Employment the People of the City are busied about. For it is the chief of their business to serve the King, so the chief of their discourse is concerning such matters. Also they talk of their own affairs, about Cattle and Husbandry. And when they meet with Outlandish-men they inquire about the Laws and Government of their Country, and if it be like theirs; and what Taxes and Duties we are bound to pay, and perform to our King, & c. And this manner of passing their leisure time they account the greatest Recreation.

In such forms there existed a public opinion which related the people to the affairs of State and which, during times of social and political crisis, could bring popular pressure to bear on the rulers, even to the extent sometimes of toppling kings and dynasties. In this context we must note the existence in precolonial society in Sri Lanka of village institutions through which disputes were settled at the local level in the presence of, and with the participation of the village community—the *gam-sabas* and *rata sabhas* or village assemblies. The mark left by these institutions on the life of the people was so strong that even during British colonial rule in the early years of the twentieth century the visit of a British civil servant to a village was the occasion for referring to him local disputes which he settled before the village audience. Leonard Woolf, a British civil servant who was the author of the best novel in English about colonial Sri Lanka, *The Village in the Jungle,* has given in his auto-biography a record of how he informally settled such a dispute, almost in the fashion of Sancho Panza, in the presence of the village community in a small and remote village in the first decade of this century.

I was holding enquiries and also conducting a sale of Crown land. . . . I was sur-rounded by a large crowd of villagers. Suddenly in the middle of the proceedings the crowd parted and an old man with one side of his face shaved and the other unshaven rushed into the ring and fell at my feet. He complained that the barber in the bazaar (and he was apparently the only barber in Walasmulla), after shav-ing one side of his face, had refused to shave the other unless he paid 50 cents. The correct price of a shave in Walasmulla was 5 cents. I sent for the barber and he appeared accompanied by some hundreds of spectators. After enquiry, I told the barber that he must complete the shave and he would be paid nothing, but if he cut the old man, he would have to pay him 50 cents. The old man was in deadly earnest, but the barber, who had the face of a rogue and a humorist, appeared to be greatly amused. We adjourned to a coconut tree in the compound of the Rest House and there the operation of shaving the old man was completed before me and an enormous crowd of spectators. The spectators were obviously delighted and amused and this revealed a characteristic of the Sinhalese which always endeared them to me.[1]

In traditional Sri Lanka society there was a whole network of modes of oral communication which served as a means of diffusing information and of

1. Leonard Woolf, *Growing,* p. 241–2.

16

shaping the thought and activity of the community. Public announcements were made by an itinerant crier, the *anaberakaraya,* who walked, beating a tom-tom to attract the attention of the people before shouting his message. On full moon days each month, marked by religious observances, virtually the entire community would gather at the local temple to worship and to hear a sermon preached by a monk. *Bana,* as this traditional form of exhortation is called, was the most powerful medium of communication shaping the moral and social values of the people in the traditional society, and it continues as a living force in Sri Lanka today, and is now regularly diffused on a national scale through the radio. At a more secular level, the traditional culture possessed a rich body of folk tales and folk songs which was passed down from generation to generation through oral tradition. A collection of traditional folk tales taken down from the lips of village narrators during the British colonial era and translated literally into English, Parker's *Folk Tales of Ceylon* attests to the vivid oral idiom of the folk tales and their fertile stock of humour, satire, romance and adventure.

The village community also possessed its own traditions of folk drama, which took many different forms—*kolam, sokari* and *nadagam.* Although the folk drama seems to have been connected in its origins with certain ritualistic functions, it developed, in colonial times, into a medium through which certain satirical attitudes on the part of the people towards the agents of colonial authority and the village exploiters could be expressed by holding them up to ridicule. Meanwhile in the last decade of the nineteenth century a new form of semi-operatic drama, the *nurtiya,* arose under Indian and Western influence to appeal to Western audiences. This latter dramatic tradition, by presenting patriotic themes drawn from the country's history, became one of the important vehicles for the expression and diffusion of nationalist ideas.

The predominantly oral character of traditional culture in Sri Lanka continued to assert itself even under modern conditions with the rise of a national movement under the leadership of a nascent middle class in the latter part of the nineteenth century. This was not surprising since literacy was still confined for the most part to the more privileged social groups. In 1881, the number of literate persons, according to national census figures, was 17.4 per cent of the population, and in 1901 it stood at 26.4 per cent. However, under the changed social conditions of the colonial era and the emergence of new political forces, there was a need for new forms of oral communication which would be capable of reaching and unifying popular opinion on a larger scale, as compared with the more local character of the older forms of oral communication. The rise of the *nurtiya,* already referred to, was in fact one reflection of this need to find new media of communication. But even more important was the growth of the mass meeting, which took place in association with the religious controversies and the temperance agitation which were some of the early manifestations of the nationalist movement.

In the latter part of the nineteenth century, the emerging nationalist movement expressed itself in its early stages as a religious and cultural renaissance, predominantly Buddhist in character, but accompanied by similar movements among Hindus and Muslims. It was natural that reaction against colonial domination should have first taken religious forms since one of the most glaring features of colonial rule was State discrimination in favour of Christianity against other religions not only in respect of the rights and privileges of religious institutions themselves but also in matters of political and public life, education and employment. The nationalist upsurge therefore sought to combat Christian influence and proselytization and to regain the lost rights of the adherents of the other religions in the country, especially of Buddhism. This campaign expressed itself in many forms, including literary polemics and newspaper agitation, which will be referred to in a later chapter; but what is relevant to the subject of this chapter is that the Buddhist revival was able to reach much wider masses of people than the literate minority because it made much more use of oral modes of communication than of the literary ones. The dominant figure in the earliest period of the Buddhist revival was a monk, Bhikku Migetuwatte Gunananda. He was described by Colonel H. S. Olcott, an American Theosophist leader who became one of the principal figures of the Buddhist renaissance in Sri Lanka, as 'the most brilliant polemical orator of the Island, the terror of missionaries'. From 1865 onwards, there was a series of public debates between Buddhists and Christians which helped in rousing mass opinion on the Buddhist side. The culmination of this series of debates was a famous public controversy at Panadura in 1873 between Bhikku Migetuwatte Gunananda and a Weslyan missionary. A contemporary account by John Capper, then editor of the *Times of Ceylon,* describes the effect that Bhikku Gunananda's oratory had on the huge crowd that was present:

Of all the weak points in Protestantism, he only touches upon those which will excite the ridicule of the people and evoke a smile of derisive contempt . . . and winds up with a brilliant peroration to which the 'great unwashed' listen with deep attention, and the accents of which ring in their ears for some minutes after delivery.

It is reported that at the end of the debate there were tumultuous cries of 'Sadhu!' (a traditional Buddhist expression of piety) from the thousands assembled, who continued shouting and demonstrating until the monk intervened to calm the crowd.

In the aftermath of the Panadura controversy and the enthusiasm it ingendered, two foreigners sympathetic to the Buddhist revival, Colonel Olcott and Madame Helena Blavatsky, arrived in Sri Lanka in 1880 to further the aims of the revival. Their message had a great potency because it was again carried to the people in both village and town through the new medium of the public meeting. Olcott described in his *Old Diary Leaves* his journeys throughout the island by travelling-cart to promote the cause of Buddhism:[1]

The arrivals at villages in the dawn; the people all clustered along the road to meet you, the bath under difficulties; early breakfast of coffee and appas; the discussion of plans with the Buddhist monks; the lecture in the open air with a great crowd of interested people. Then come the spreading of printed subscription sheets on a table, the registering of names, the sale of Buddhist tracts; the goodbyes, tom-toms, waving of flags, and cries of Sadhu! Sadhu! and the resumption of the journey . . . and so on and so on, day after day.

In the wake of Bhikku Migetuwatte Gunananda and Colonel Olcott came a new generation of Buddhist reformers and campaigners, of whom the most militant were Anagarika Dharmapala (1864–1933) and Walisinha Harischandra (1877–1913). It is significant that both of them were powerful and magnetic orators who again used the mass meeting as their principal mode of expression to stir nationalist and Buddhist consciousness.

A by-product of the Buddhist revival was the temperance movement. Originally religious in character (since one of the five precepts of Buddhism is abstinence from alcohol), the movement rapidly developed an anticolonial character since alcohol was regarded as a foreign vice strengthened by the colonial régime through its excise laws. The temperance movement reached its peaks in the years 1903–5 and 1911–14. The movement developed the institution of the public meeting to a hitherto unprecedented extent; for instance, the best organized temperance society in the country is reported to have drawn crowds of 20,000 and over to its meetings in a rural area.

The Buddhist revival, as has already been mentioned, had its parallel among the Hindu and Muslim communities in the country. The leading figure among the Hindus of this period was Arumuga Navalar (1822–79) who was the pioneer of polemical public oratory in the Tamil language and therefore played in the northern (predominantly Tamil) area of the island a role similar to that fulfilled by the charismatic orators who have already been referred to in the predominantly Sinhalese and Buddhist south.

The public mass meeting, which had originally arisen as a religio-political mode of communication, took on a more definitely secular social and political character with the rise of the urban working class and the trade union movement in the twentieth century. Indeed, some of the principal figures of the Buddhist revival had also been friends of trade unionism; and A. E. Goonesinha (1891–1967), under whom the trade-union movement achieved its first signal victories in the 1920s, began his career as a follower of Anagarika Dharmapala. One of the most important factors behind A. E. Goonesinha's ascent in trade unionism and working-class politics was that he brought through his public speaking a new language that fired the working class with enthusiasm—a language of popular invective against the

1. H. S. Olcott, *Old Diary Leaves*, p. 305.

colonial rulers, police and employers that removed the workers' fear of authority.

Until 1931, however, national politics continued to be hemmed in by an elitist framework since the colonial legislature was based on a limited fran-chise. In that year, however, a new constitution under which the colonial rulers granted universal adult franchise became effective, and gave new scope to the institution of the mass meeting as a means of influencing public opinion. The first political group to exploit the new opportunities to use the medium of the mass meeting were a Marxist party formed in 1935, the Lanka Sama Samaja Party, which rapidly took over the leadership of the urban working class from Goonesinha. They too possessed a fiery orator in Philip Gunawardena, one of the first left-wing members to be elected to the legislature.

The growth of the mass meeting as a means of influencing public opin-ion was temporarily halted by the Second World War, during which the colonial régime severely restricted democratic rights of assembly and speech. However, the need for communication through public speaking expressed itself in surreptitious forms: during the war years funeral orations (which were not banned) became one of the principal means of ventilating critical opinions on public affairs. With the end of the war, the resumption of political life, and the achievement of political independence in 1948, the mass meeting came fully into its own as the main medium of public com-munication and of influencing opinion, and has remained so ever since. In every general election, the political fortunes of the contending parties have been determined principally by their ability to sway mass opinion by the cam-paigns they have conducted through many hundreds of meetings up and down the country. It is again not without significance that the most decisive change in the country's recent political history—the transfer of power in 1956 from the United National Party, which had ruled since independence, to a coalition headed by the Sri Lanka Freedom Party—was the outcome of an election campaign in which the dominant figure was one of the most skilful and eloquent public speakers Sri Lanka has produced, S. W. R. D. Bandaranaike (1900–59).

The continued predominance of the public meeting as the main medium of electoral politics can be related to the absence in Sri Lanka of television, the exclusion of election campaigning from the State-controlled radio, and the weakness of the press as a means of influencing popular political opinion, for reasons that will be examined in the next chapter. But it is not only in a pre-election period that the mass meeting serves as the most influential medium of public communication on political questions. It occupies this position at all times.

This phenomenon poses a question of fundamental importance. It was inevitable, in the traditional society of Sri Lanka, that oral modes of com-munication should have been dominant since literacy was then restricted to a minority and the means of diffusing information, knowledge and opinion by the written word were scanty. Since the adoption of universal free education as a State policy in 1945, however, there has been a phenomenal growth in literacy to a level almost without parallel in Asia (according to the last census, the number of literate persons was 78 per cent of the population). Simultaneously, there has been a rapid growth of the printing press and of the circulation of newspapers and other publications. It might have been expected that this development would be accompanied by the supersession in importance of oral modes of communication by written ones. This indeed has been the normal result of the rise of literate cultures elsewhere. Yet this has not happened in Sri Lanka. The next chapter will seek to discover the reasons.

3 The press in Sri Lanka

Although Sinhala, the language of the majority of the population in Sri Lanka, and Tamil, the language of the principal racial minority, both have a long literary history—older than that of any living European language—their literatures were originally handed down in oral tradition, carved on stone, or written down in manuscript on the leaves of the talipot palm. The introduction of the printing press and the first stages of its growth in Sri Lanka were a product of colonial rule. The earliest printed literature to be produced in the indigenous languages was part of the Christian missionary endeavour fostered by the colonial régimes. The first Sinhala book to be printed was a book of prayer, containing the Lord's Prayer, morning and night prayers, grace before and after meals, twelve articles of the Creed, and the Ten Commandments. It was printed in 1737 at the printing press of the Dutch Government in the island. A Sinhala version of the New Testament was translated and published, also in Dutch times, in 1780, and the first complete translation of the Bible into Sinhala appeared under British rule in 1817.

For the first newspaper Sri Lanka had to wait until British times. Shortly after the British occupation in 1796 of the maritime provinces of the island, under the governorship of the Hon. Frederic North, the first newspaper appeared in English in 1802. This was the *Ceylon Government Gazette,* and its first issue on 15 March, 1802, carried the following announcement:

His Excellency the Governor, being of opinion that great convenience would arise to the Public if all Government Orders and Notifications were made known and circulated through the medium of News-paper, has been pleased to direct that a Prospectus of such a Paper should be prepared and published as follows: Viz. Prospectus of a Weekly Newspaper to be called 'The Ceylon Government Gazette'. This Paper is to contain Proclamations, General Orders, Government Advertisements, Judicial and all other notifications that it may be deemed to be beneficial for the Public to be informed of. Also the advertisements of Individuals announcing Public or Private Sales, Notices of Lost Goods, Arrival and Departure of Ships, Births, Marriages and Deaths, and all other matters that may with propriety come under the name of Public Advertisement.... The Paper will be published every Monday before Twelve O'clock in order that it may be despatched by Post on the day of publication and it will go Free of Postage to all parts of the British Territories in Ceylon.

The *Government Gazette* continues to be published to this day, and now serves exclusively the function of carrying government notifications in the three principal languages of the island. When it first appeared, however, the *Gazette* contained in addition to these notifications, literary and political contributions, descriptions of marriages, obituary articles, and even merry quips. Thus, the *Gazette* at that time fulfilled some of the functions of a general newspaper, in the absence of any other.

The first attempt to produce a newspaper independent of government began with the arrival in the island of Sir Robert Wilmot Horton as Governor. With his encouragement a weekly newspaper called the *Colombo Journal* was launched in 1832. But the British Government did not approve of this enterprise, and the newspaper ceased publication in 1833, on the orders of the authorities in London.

But the demand for an independent newspaper had been created, and the gap left by the closing down of the *Colombo Journal* was soon filled by the appearance of the *Colombo Observer and Commercial Advertiser* in 1834. It was founded by British merchants in Colombo, and changing hands over the next 140 years, it has continued to be published down to the present day. Under the editorship of Dr Christopher Elliott, an ardent Irishman, it became an organ for outspoken criticism of the government. Dr Elliott was succeeded in 1859 as editor by A. M. Ferguson, under whom the newspaper became an even more influential voice of progress. Fundamentally, the paper expressed the views and interests of the British commercial and agricultural interests in the island, but indirectly it served to reflect some of the needs and grievances against the colonial bureaucracy of the vast mass of the people of the country, who had no such organ of public expression of their own. The growing distribution and influence of the paper is signified by the fact that in 1867 the *Colombo Observer* became the *Ceylon Observer*.

There were several English-language newspapers which enjoyed more or less brief existences during the early British period, but of the newspapers started during this time, the only other one besides the *Observer* which has survived down to the present day is the *Ceylon Times* (now the *Times of Ceylon*) begun in 1846. It was founded exclusively for the furtherance of sectional mercantile European interests, and continued to remain the organ of these interests until it passed into Ceylonese hands in the 1940s.

The value of an independent press at a time when there were no institutions of democratic government was revealed in one of the major crises of the early British period—the rebellion of 1848. This originated as an agitation against oppressive taxes, but the administration panicked, declared martial law, and shot many innocent people. In this situation the *Observer* was the voice of liberalism; it agitated for a full and impartial inquiry, which the Governor, Lord Torrington, did his best to resist. But the *Observer*'s campaign succeeded in inducing the British Government to appoint a high-powered Select Committee of the British Parliament as a result of whose inquiry the Governor and several of his associates were recalled.

In the second half of the nineteenth century the growth of a national movement, associated with the rise of a middle class who wanted a share in running the affairs of the country, was reflected in the rise of newspapers representing indigenous interests as distinct from those of British planting and mercantile groups. The first such newspaper was the *Examiner*. Although started by a few Colombo merchants in 1846 as a British mercantile organ, with a change of ownership in 1859, it came under the influence of C. A. Lorenz, a Dutch descendant, who was a distinguished lawyer, writer and politician and represented the interests of the Burghers (as those of Dutch descent were called) in the Legislative Council. A syndicate headed by Lorenz bought the paper (which was renamed the *Ceylon Examiner*); the other members of the syndicate were three Sinhalese, Sir Harry Dias, James de Alwis, a great Oriental scholar, and J. A. Dunuwille, a distinguished advocate. The newspaper, which existed till 1900, was accepted as a Ceylonese organ which voiced the views of indigenous opinion. Lorenz, at the time he took over the newspaper, had expressed the hope that be would be able to 'prove after all that Ceylon has arrived at a position when her children can speak out for themselves'. Other newspapers were to take up the tradition begun by Lorenz: the *Ceylon Independent,* founded by Hector Van Cuylenberg, Burgher member of the Legislative Council, in 1888, the *Ceylon Standard,* started in 1908 by a group of wealthy Sinhalese, and the *Morning Leader,* which was established by another group of Sinhalese land-owning families to take over from the *Ceylon Standard* when it went into liquidation.

The newspapers to which reference has so far been made were all published in English, and therefore necessarily reached only the British planting and mercantile groups and the small privileged native élite in Sri Lanka who read English. In the indigenous languages Tamil journalism preceded that in the Sinhala language. The first journalistic venture, in the Tamil-speaking northern part of the island was the *Morning Star,* a bimonthly Tamil journal founded in 1841. A great impetus to Tamil journalism was given by Arumuga Navalar, the leader of the Hindu revival referred to in the last chapter. In 1849 he established a printing press in Jaffna, from which poured a stream of tracts and pamphlets expounding Hinduism and defending it against missionary attacks, in a language that the ordinary man could understand.

However, with the growth of the nationalist and Buddhist revival in the Sinhala-speaking south in the latter part of the nineteenth century, Sinhala journalism began to come into its own. The first Sinhala newspaper, the *Lakminipahana,* a weekly, was founded in 1862. The Catholics in the island had already established their own Sinhala newspaper, the *Gnanartha Pradeepaya,* in 1867. The Buddhist revivalists therefore felt the need for their own organ. The visit of Colonel Olcott and Madame Blavatsky (referred to in Chapter 2) in 1880 became the occasion for the formation of the Buddhist Theosophical Society, which became the spearhead of the Buddhist revivalist movement. In the same year the society decided to found its own Sinhala newspaper, the *Sarasavisandaresa,* which began publication in

December 1880 as a weekly. By 1887 the increasing demand led to its conversion to a biweekly. Its main contributor became Anagarika Dharmapala, the militant Buddhist reformer whose work has been described in the previous chapter. The journal criticized the policies of the colonial régime and exposed misdeeds of government officials. Its editor, H. S. Perera, was prosecuted for libel on several occasions because of his attacks on persons in high places. Another Sinhala newspaper followed in the wake of the *Sarasavisandaresa;* this was the *Sinhala Bauddhaya* (founded in 1906) to which also Anagarika Dharmapala contributed a regular column in which he wrote in forceful language on topical social and political issues. The influence of these newspapers is indicated by the fact that during an outbreak of rioting in 1915, both of them were banned by the colonial government.

However, it is evident from the fact that the literacy rate by 1911 had still reached only 26.4 per cent that even these nationalist newspapers published in the Sinhala language could reach only a minority, largely middle-class readership. The next phase in the growth of popular newspapers in Sri Lanka was to be pioneered by D. R. Wijewardena (1886–1950), the most dynamic figure in the history of Sri Lanka's newspaper industry. It was he who established the first large-scale newspaper enterprise to be owned by interests of Sri Lanka, and who in new social and political circumstances created the first newspapers to enjoy a mass circulation.

D. R. Wijewardene, who began his public life as a lawyer, entered the newspaper industry by buying the *Dinamina,* a Sinhala daily newspaper. A few years later, in 1918, he bought the goodwill and plant of an English-language newspaper, the *Ceylonese,* which had been founded five years earlier by other hands, and was now bankrupt. He used the newly acquired press to found an English-language daily newspaper, the *Ceylon Daily News,* which, since English was still the language of the social and political élite, was to become and to remain until his death the most prestigious and influential newspaper in the country. In 1923, he also acquired the *Ceylon Observer,* the oldest of the surviving English-language newspapers in the island. By the time he died, in 1950, the newspaper business he established, the Associated Newspapers of Ceylon Ltd, had grown into the largest and most successful combine of its kind in the country, producing by that time three daily morning newspapers (one in each of the languages Sinhala, Tamil and English), one evening newspaper in English, and three Sunday newspapers, one of which, a Sinhala newspaper, the *Silumina,* enjoyed the highest circulation for any newspaper in South-East Asia.

Wijewardene's achievement as a newspaper publisher was made possible by a number of factors. One of the most important of these was that he entered the field of newspaper publishing at a time when new impulses towards constitutional reform and the desire for a greater share in the management of the affairs of the country for the representatives of the people (meaning in practice at this time the land-owning, business and professional élite) were beginning to be felt. Wijewardene's newspapers, the *Ceylon Daily News* in particular, became from the beginning the organ of this movement towards constitutional reform, which was to culminate in 1948 in the peaceful transfer of power by the United Kingdom to the elected representatives of the people. Appropriately enough, the first issue of the *Ceylon Daily News* in 1918 carried on its front page a message from Sir Ponnambalam Arunachalam, a member of the Legislative Council and a leader of the reform movement, which opened with these words:

The *Ceylon Daily News* is fortunate in the time of its birth. New forces are at work among us, a new era is dawning for our country. She needs the devoted services of all her children, and will, I am confident, find none more zealous in her cause than the new Daily.

Particularly after the grant of universal franchise in 1931, Wijewardene worked closely hand in hand with the political leaders whose policy was to achieve independence by peaceful negotiation with the United Kingdom, and used popular agitation only as a means of bringing pressure to bear on the colonial régime in the furtherance of this end. In particular, he shared an essential community of outlook with D. S. Senanayake, who was in 1948 to win independence by constitutional means and to become the first Prime Minister of the new Dominion. Since the national movement in Sri Lanka was to remain, right up to independence and for a few years after, largely dominated by an élite, the common aims which Wijewardene shared with them was at this time a source of strength for his newspapers. At the same time the fact that his newspapers criticized the colonial bureaucracy and pressed for a growing share of power for the representatives of the people gave his papers a popularity which enabled them soon to eclipse their main competitor, the *Times of Ceylon,* which continued until independence to be the organ of British planting and mercantile interests.

The fact that Wijewardene's papers reflected the new currents of political reform would not, however, have sufficed to build the success of his enterprise if he had not also been a highly efficient and far-sighted publisher, businessman and manager. He brought to newspaper publishing in Sri Lanka the most modern techniques of journalism, news-gathering, layout and display current at the time. Further, his integrity was respected even by those who disagreed with his policies. Although he supported through his newspapers the policies of the leadership of the national movement for constitutional reform, he dealt with them as equals and not as a dependant. In order to retain his independence of action, he regulated even his personal life in keeping with this end, as has been stated by his daughter in some reminiscences included in a biography of him:[1]

As he became more and more absorbed in the newspaper he realised that friendships and even relationships would have to be sacrificed if they interfered with the policies which he thought were best for the newspapers and the country. The

1. H. A. J. Hulugalle, *The Life and Times of D. R. Wijewardene,* p. 244.

comments and criticisms of the newspapers could be effective only if he himself was above suspicion, and this principle he rigidly maintained. He cut himself off from all political and social organisations and maintained only a small circle of his intimate friends.

Two events which took place in Wijewardene's lifetime were to become decisive not only for the future of the enterprise he founded but also for the larger social and political history of the country. In 1931, the British Government brought into effect in Sri Lanka a new constitution that granted universal franchise, a right that was at that time unique in any British colony. In itself, the grant of this right did not immediately disturb the elitist structure of political life, for when the first elections to the new legislature, the State Council, were held in 1931, a still predominantly uneducated and politically unawakened electorate tended to follow where their social betters led them. However, the existence of a legislature whose members were dependent on the popular vote created a pressure for popular measures of social welfare. The most important of these measures, and one which was to be far reaching in its social consequences, was the adoption by the government of the principle of universal free education. Although in 1945 when this principle was adopted, only a minority of the country's children and youth were going to school, the very acceptance of the principle led to steadily increasing popular pressures for educational facilities throughout the country. In 1943 when the proposal for free education was first mooted by a Special Committee on Education, the government's expenditure on education was 24.8 million rupees; already in 1947, only two years after the implementation of the proposal, it had risen to 84.7 million rupees. This was only the beginning of a steady expansion of educational facilities and the progressive eradication of illiteracy at a tempo unparalleled in the South-East Asian region.

This rapid rise in literacy should have made possible in Sri Lanka a considerable expansion not only in the circulation but also in the social influence and power of the press. It should have led to a situation in which the printed word, and the newspaper in particular as the most broad-based of the mass media, should have displaced the older oral traditions as the dominant mode of communication. In fact, circulation did expand rapidly, especially of the Sinhala newspapers which now found an entirely new readership in fresh strata of the population which was becoming literate. This fact is signified not only by the expansion in the circulation of previously existing newspapers, but also by the appearance of new Sinhala daily newspapers—the *Lankadipa,* a morning paper founded by the Times group in 1947, the *Janata,* an evening newspaper begun by Lake House (as the Wijewardene group was popularly known) in 1953, and the *Davasa* and *Savasa,* a morning and evening paper respectively, launched by a new enterprise, the Independent Newspapers Ltd, founded in 1961.

However, the growth in the number of newspapers and in their circulation was not accompanied by a corresponding rise in their influence over social and political thinking. This was because the newspapers in the post-

27

independence period were isolated from the new social forces that were emerging to challenge the dominance of the old land-owning, mercantile and professional élites, tied to a colonial way of life, who had dominated the national life up to that time. These new social forces were principally the nationalist-minded rural middle class and rural intelligentsia, carrying with them broad masses of the peasantry on the one hand, and the urban working class and lower middle class on the other.

The first major political outcome of these developments was the defeat at the general election of 1956 of the United National Party which had ruled the country since independence, but whose strength in Parliament was now reduced from seventy-five to eight seats, and the coming to power of a coalition headed by the Sri Lanka Freedom Party and led by S. W. R. D. Bandaranaike. What is relevant for the purposes of this study is that the 1956 general election demonstrated conclusively the meagreness of the influence on popular opinion exercised by the press. In the pre-election period the press, which was now virtually a monopoly of two powerful newspaper groups, the Lake House and Times groups, threw its strength entirely behind the ruling party. Lake House had in fact always been associated politically with the government; the Times group had, in the immediate post-independence period, played a certain critical role, but as the general election approached, it submerged these differences and threw its weight too behind the government. The support given to the government by these two groups which dominated the newspaper field, owning all the large-circulation dailies and weeklies, extended not only to editorial comment but also to the presentation of news in a manner conducive to the interests of the government. Since the radio was also State controlled, this meant that all the major mass media were ranged on one side. This, however, did not prevent public opinion from turning decisively against the ruling party. What was particularly striking was that this major shift in popular opinion found no reflection in the dominant mass media up to the very day of the general election. It was quite evident, therefore, that the molecular movements in public thinking were transmitted by means quite other than the mass media. It was through the mass meetings of the pre-election period as well as through interpersonal communication in village and work place that the decisive changes in public opinion were brought about. Oral modes of communication prevailed over the mass media and the printed word, not only because these were the traditional means of communication but also because the monopolistic character of the press and its isolation from the new social forces created a credibility gap that deprived it of influence. The pattern of the general election of 1956 was to be repeated in subsequent general elections in July 1960 and in 1970, where again the outcome of the elections, as determined by the popular vote, was entirely contrary to the direction in which the press sought to exert its influence.

The general election of 1956 began a new period in the relations between the press and the State in Sri Lanka, since for the first time there was an elected government which did not enjoy, as previous régimes did, the whole-hearted support of the major newspaper groups. It was also after 1956 that the government for the first time expressed its awareness of the fact that the structure of the press in Sri Lanka constituted a monopoly by a few powerful groups. In an address to the Press Association of Ceylon in 1959, Prime Minister, S. W. R. D. Bandaranaike, referring to 'the responsibility of the Press in guiding public opinion and in reflecting public opinion', said:

Very true, that responsibility is particularly important in a country like this where we have something approaching a Press monopoly. One of the most unhealthy features in this democracy of Sri Lanka is this existence of what in fact amounts to press dictatorship, a Press monopoly.

Mr Bandaranaike further clarifying the issue said:

It amounts to almost a monopoly which is most unhealthy in any democratic country because far worse than political dictatorship is a situation amounting to the dictatorship of a Press monopoly. In various ways, this Press monopoly, if it does not approve of a Government elected to power by the votes of the people can, by various exaggerations, distortions and misrepresentations, create an almost impossible position for such a Government. Therefore, the position arises that only a Government of which this Press chooses to approve, can function satisfactorily.

He also added that a dictatorship of the Press was one of the worst types of dictatorship.

A political dictator, well, there you know where he is, so that you know where you are, but with Press dictatorship you do not know. The ordinary public do not know where they are with Press dictatorship. A political leader makes his speech. They know well that it is his view. But when something appears in a newspaper, people do not attribute it to an individual. It is something impersonal and therefore has a greater force.
    There are various methods by which a newspaper concern can put forward ideas and views in a way that does not become apparent to the reading public. If I say something they know that it is my view. They know what value to attach to it. If my good friend, Dr N. M. Perera (Leader of the Opposition) says something, they know that it is Dr N. M. Perera's view and they know what value to attach to that.
    But in a newspaper, by various methods of omission, of commission, of a slight twist here, a slight distortion there, by letters addressed to the Press usually under the title 'Pro Bono Publico', generally manufactured in the Press itself, by various articles and by various editorial stratagems, a wrong impression can be created in the minds of the public.

However, S. W. R. D. Bandaranaike died in 1959 before he could give his mind to any steps to solve this problem. Until 1964 there was no attempt at direct State intervention in the press, except for brief periods of censorship during times of civil commotion, when the government assumed temporary emergency powers. In 1960 the government of Mrs Srimavo Bandaranaike had announced in its first statement of policy that it would introduce a Bill to convert the two major newspaper groups, the Associated Newspapers of Ceylon Ltd (Lake House) and the Times of Ceylon Ltd, into public corporations with broad-based ownership as a means of breaking up monopolistic ownership of the press. However, no action was taken on this proposal until the latter stages of the government's lifetime. Meanwhile in 1963 the government had appointed a Commission of Inquiry to report on a wide range of matters connected with the structure and functioning of the press. These included the following:

The structure, ownership and control of undertakings publishing newspapers and periodicals, of news agencies and of feature syndicates, with particular regard to the degree of concentration of ownership and control prevailing in the newspaper business.

The extent to which the concentration of such ownership and control operates to the prejudice of the free expression of opinion or the accurate presentation of news, or is otherwise detrimental to the best interests of the public.

The measures that should be adopted to break up the monopoly of the press and the influence and control exercised by international monopolies connected with the supply, distribution and control of news.

The commission in its report issued in 1964 held that

by reason of the concentration of the ownership of the four principal newspaper companies in the hands of four families and a few individuals, there is a definite monopoly of the Press.

It went on to say:[1]

With the grant of Independence . . . the political power passed into the hands of the masses but the economic control continued to remain in the hands of a privileged minority. The Press has proved to be one of the very few powerful bastions still in the possession of that minority.

The commission made a detailed examination of the contents of newspapers in order to demonstrate that press monopoly had led to partisanship, distortion and slanting of news. Its principal recommendations for the correction of these ills was first, the break-up of the existing concentration of ownership, and establishment of newspapers owned by co-operatives and broad-based public companies; secondly, the establishment of a statutory Press Council, 'not with the slightest intention of curbing the freedom of the Press thereby, but in order to preserve its real independence undiminished'. The council was to have wide powers to lay down codes of ethics for journalists and newspapers, to order corrections and apologies where biased and distorted news had been published, and to exercise other regulatory functions in the public interest. The commission, however, emphasized that the council should:[2]

1. *Final Report of the Press Commission,* Para. 20, Colombo.
2. ibid., Para. 221.

Recognise the fundamental right of a newspaper to present news without slanting, distorting or suppressing; the right to express forthright views on any matter, irrespective of the personalities involved, must be jealously guarded; not only individual officers but the Government itself, when the necessity arises, should be open to severe criticism of a legitimate nature; the expression of political and other views, provided they are not scandalous or penalised by law, should be permitted without restriction; and generally the growth of newspapers should be encouraged.

Following the publication of the Press Commission's report, the government announced in its policy statement for the next session of Parliament its proposal to introduce a Bill for the formation of a public corporation to take over the Lake House group of newspapers. During the debate on this policy statement, however, the government was defeated as a result of a section of its members crossing over to the opposition on this issue. The question of press monopoly thus went into abeyance for six years—until the return to power at the general election of 1970 of a new United Front Government headed by Mrs Sirimavo Bandaranaike. In 1973, this government introduced two Bills, which were passed by Parliament, relating to the press in Sri Lanka. One Bill was for the establishment of a Press Council, and the other for the conversion of the Lake House group of newspapers into a public corporation.

The Sri Lanka Press Council Law, as adopted by Parliament, creates a council consisting of seven members. One of them is the Director of Information (*ex-officio*). Of the six other members to be appointed by the President of the Republic of Sri Lanka, one is to represent working journalists; and one is to represent the interests of the employees of newspaper businesses. Every member of the council (other than the Director of Information) holds office for three years, but can be removed from office by the President during that period, if he becomes ineligible by becoming a Member of the National State Assembly, if he becomes permanently incapable of performing his functions as a member, or if he commits any act which in the opinion of the President is of a fraudulent or illegal character, or is likely to damage the interests of the council. The objects of the council are defined as follows:

1. To ensure the freedom of the press in Sri Lanka, to prevent abuses of that freedom, and to safeguard the character of the Sri Lanka press in accordance with the highest professional standards.
2. To ensure that newspapers shall be free to publish as news true statements of facts, and any comments based upon true statements of facts.
3. To ensure on the part of newspapers and journalists the maintenance of high standards of journalistic ethics, and to foster a due sense of both the rights and responsibilities of citizenship.
4. To improve methods of recruitment, education, welfare and training in the profession of journalism.
5. To promote a proper functional relation among all sections engaged in the production or publication of newspapers, and the establishment of common services for the supply and dissemination of news as may from time to time appear to be desirable.

6. To undertake research into the use and needs of the press, to keep under review developments likely to restrict the supply of information of public interest and importance and developments in the Sri Lanka press which may tend towards concentration or monopoly, and to suggest appropriate remedial measures in relation thereto.
7. To advise the government on any matter pertaining to the regulation and conduct of newspapers.

The council was given wide powers to conduct inquiries into complaints regarding publication of untrue, distorted or improper statements, pictures or other matter, as well as complaints regarding professional misconduct and breach of journalistic ethics, and to order corrections and apologies and to censure newspapers, publishers and journalists where such complaints were proved to be justified. The law also created penal offences in respect of the publication in any newspaper of profane, defamatory obscene matter and unauthorized publication of Cabinet proceedings and decisions, official secrets pertaining to defence, or of matter likely to lead to the creation of shortages or windfall profits or other adverse consequences to the economy of the country. The law also made it an offence to publish in any newspaper any proposal or other matter, alleged to be under consideration by any Minister or any Ministry or the Government, when it is false that such proposal or matter is under consideration by such Minister, Ministry or by the Government.

Although the Press Council Law gave a wide range of powers and functions to the council, and also restricted by penal sanctions the publication of certain kinds of matter regarded as undesirable, it is not so much this law as the changes in the ownership and structure of the press since 1973 that have altered the character of newspapers in Sri Lanka. Although the press council is empowered to exercise many different functions, in practice it has confined its activity since its establishment in 1973 to inquiring into complaints made by aggrieved individuals or organizations against this or that item in a newspaper, and ordering corrections or apologies wherever it has upheld such complaints.

More far-reaching in its consequences for the press in Sri Lanka has been the other Bill introduced in 1973 relating to this field: the Associated Newspapers of Ceylon Ltd (Special Provisions) Bill. This Bill provided for the conversion of the Lake House group into a public corporation by the compulsory sale of the majority of the shares held by the existing shareholders. By the carrying into effect of its provisions, the former monopoly control held by the Wijewardene family has been broken up. Ownership has been diffused among many individuals and organizations, but since a large proportion of the shares have been sold to government corporations and other such institutions, the result of the change in ownership has been said to concentrate power in the hands of the government. It is expected that the press council will take appropriate action to maintain the balance in the matter of reporting news.

Meanwhile, in 1974, the government, acting under emergency powers assumed during the insurrection of 1971, closed down one of the three major newspaper groups, the Independent Newspapers Ltd, which was engaged in a vociferous and patently unjustified anti-government campaign, both in comment and in news reporting. In 1975, a change of ownership by purchase took place in the other major newspaper group in the country—the Times of Ceylon Ltd. This group still continues under private ownership.

Within the last few years, therefore, there has been a complete change in the character of the press in Sri Lanka. State intervention has brought about a fundamental change in the ownership and control of the largest newspaper group in the country, and has interrupted the functioning of another of the major groups, while the policies of the other remaining group have been re-aligned by passing into new hands. The other newspapers which continue to function outside this ambit are nearly all organs of political parties, most of which enjoy relatively smaller circulations as well as restricted sizes in number of pages and space. The shortages and high prices of newsprint which have prevailed during recent years make it difficult for small newspapers without large capital investment and without State advertisements of flourish, and make it unlikely that any newspaper group capable of competing with the established groups will emerge in the near future.

4 The radio in Sri Lanka

The history of sound broadcasting in Sri Lanka goes back to 1923, when some experiments in this field were carried out by the Ceylon Telegraph Department, only three years after broadcasting had begun in Europe. Shortly after an official committee was appointed to report on the introduction of broadcasting and the nature of the control that should be exercised over it. The committee recommended that broadcasting should be under State control though not necessarily operated by the State, and under normal conditions should be left to private enterprise. They proposed, however, the establishment of a Broadcasting Board, headed by the Postmaster-General, in all matters connected with wireless and broadcasting.

The recommendations of the committee were accepted by the colonial government, and transmission begun on an experimental basis in 1924, leading to the inauguration of a regular broadcasting service in 1925, making Sri Lanka the first British colony to provide such a service. But in one important respect, the government departed in practice from the recommendations of the 1923 committee. Broadcasting was never thrown open to private enterprise but became a monopoly of the State and continued to be so after independence. However, the controlling authority which exercised the direction and administration of authority on behalf of the State has varied in the course of the history of broadcasting in Sri Lanka. Originally it was the Postmaster-General, who functioned with the help of an advisory board.

Although Sri Lanka entered the field of broadcasting very early, the growth and development of the new mass medium were very slow. A report produced by the Special Committee on Broadcasting in Ceylon in 1941 stated:[1]

Taking up the comparison of the figures relating to the steady progress of broadcasting in India during the last four or five years, we regret to note that there has been little, if any progress, made by Ceylon during the same period. . . . The outlook in Ceylon appears to have been guided by an effort to balance the income and expenditure of the Broadcasting Service.

The revenue to the government in respect of broadcasting came at this time entirely from licence fees and customs duty on receiving sets. At the time the

1. *Report of the Special Committee on Broadcasting in Ceylon*, Para. 34, Colombo, 1941.

34

committee reported there were 10,089 licence holders. Apart from the bureaucratic approach of balancing income and expenditure referred to in the report, there were several other factors which slowed down the development of broadcasting in its early phases. Listening was concentrated mainly in urban areas where electric power was available. The battery-operated sets of the time were cumbersome, and recharging them in many areas of the country involved transporting them over long distances. The programmes were directed mainly towards English-educated listeners, and this minority, who represented the more urbanized and affluent sections of the population, formed the greater part of the listening public at that time. A further limitation on the popularity of broadcasting was that the technical facilities available (a single medium wave transmitter of 3.5 kW power) permitted good regular reception only in a small part of the island.

On the technical side, broadcasting in Sri Lanka received a considerable fillip from the establishment in the island of the South-East Asia Command (SEAC) radio station by the British military services during the Second World War. At the end of the war, the Government of Sri Lanka negotiated with the British authorities to take over the equipment of SEAC radio, including its powerful transmitters, and this was transferred to the Sri Lanka Government (now independent) in 1949. Simultaneously with this, the government decided to constitute for the first time a separate department to run the broadcasting services, and this was set up in 1949 under the name of Radio Ceylon under a Director-General of Broadcasting. In the following year, the government approved the inauguration of a Commercial Service of Radio Ceylon to broadcast sponsored programmes including commercial advertising. The main argument advanced in favour of commercial broadcasting was that it would provide a plentiful source of income which could finance the development of cultural, informational and educational broadcasting in the regular national service of Radio Ceylon. This forecast has proved to be correct as far as the potentialities of income were concerned, and by the end of the second decade of commercial broadcasting the commercial service was earning over 7 million rupees a year. However, there has been a recurrent controversy on the question whether commercial broadcasting has led to a debasement of taste, and the Commission of Inquiry on Broadcasting in 1953 recommended the closing down of the commercial service, and its replacement by controlled advertisements during specified hours. This recommendation was not, however, accepted by the government of the day or by any subsequent government.

Although at the time of the 1953 commission, the number of licensed radio sets had increased to 92,341, the commission still felt this to be inadequate in a population of over 8 million, compared with figures not only in the advanced countries but also in developing countries like Cuba, Brazil and Lebanon.

Up to this time broadcasting in the English language and Western-oriented programmes continued to dominate Radio Ceylon, in allocation of both time and resources, as compared with Sinhala and Tamil broadcasting.

35

(In 1953 services directed to the Western-oriented listener occupied 49.75 hours per week as compared with 43.5 hours for Sinhala and 39 hours for Tamil listeners.) This disproportion, which was a hangover from a colonial culture, was not corrected till after 1956.

Another commission of inquiry, meeting in 1966, recommended that Radio Ceylon, which from its inception had been a government department, should be converted into a broadcasting corporation:[1]

Listeners demand an efficient service with programmes of high quality, including legitimate controversy and objective news bulletins, for which the broadcasting authority should take full responsibility. A broadcasting service does not flourish under the heavy hand of departmentalism.

With the aim of giving the radio greater independence and autonomy, the commission proposed the establishment of a broadcasting corporation on the model not exactly of the British Broadcasting Corporation (BBC) but of the New Zealand Broadcasting Corporation (NZBC). While taking note of 'the fears that a Board oppointed by the Government of the day will be heavily weighted with party sympathizers and men who have in their time served the State and are due for some reward', the commission found ground for optimism in the following considerations:[2]

A Government which entrusts a powerful medium of communication to unworthy hands will discredit itself. We are aware that whatever we may suggest to prevent such a disaster will be of no avail under a dictatorship or other totalitarian government. No fences can be erected against the arbitrary use of power. An enlightened democratic government will, on the other hand, take good care to place in worthy hands an instrument that can promote national unity, expedite economic development, encourage the arts, improve taste, liberalise education and make the nation happy by providing clean and lively entertainment.

With these sanguine expectations the Ceylon Broadcasting Corporation (now the Sri Lanka Broadcasting Corporation) was set up in 1966 by an Act of Parliament, with a five-member board nominated by the minister in charge of information and broadcasting. It is within this structure that the organizational control and direction of broadcasting has been exercised during the last ten years.

Following this brief historical survey of broadcasting in Sri Lanka, it is necessary to assess the contribution made by this medium to national development.

Radio broadcasting in Sri Lanka began with the potential advantage that as an auditory medium, it could have functioned as an extension of the oral tradition of communication in Sri Lanka, and did not suffer from

---

1. *Report of the Commission on Broadcasting and Information*, Para. 59, Colombo. 1966.
2. ibid., Para. 67.

dependence on literacy which was a barrier to the growth of the press in its early years. It is true that, as has been mentioned above, there were certain technical difficulties in the popularization of radio in its first stages, but the most important of these has been overcome by the invention of the transistor-operated radio set, which has brought radio listening within the reach of listeners in rural as well as urban areas.

Although this and other social developments such as improvement of peasant and working-class incomes have led to a steady increase in the diffusion of radio sets among the population (455,368 licensed sets in 1974), this growth has not been paralleled by a corresponding increase in the power of radio as a means of communication. The radio remains in Sri Lanka for the most part what it has been since its inception—a medium of entertainment and a source of information rather than of meaningful and effective communication on questions of social and political importance affecting the community.

Successive governments in Sri Lanka were slow to realize the valuable potentialities of the radio as a medium of mass communication. Before 1956, governments in power paid little attention to the radio except as a medium of entertainment and routine news-broadcasting, because the governments of that time had the press wholly on their side and therefore relied on the newspapers as their main medium of publicity and propaganda.

After 1956, governments which were faced with a hostile press tended to build up the radio as a medium to express their own point of view and to build up their own image. This was an understandable reaction, particularly in periods when an elected government was faced with irresponsible opposition from the Press, but its result has been to make the State-owned radio a one-sided and partisan medium, detracting from its effectiveness as a means of influencing public opinion. As in the case of the newspapers referred to in the previous chapter, the credibility gap has been damaging to the acceptability of news and views broadcast by the radio.

As with the press, general elections have served to prove the resistance of public opinion to partisan propaganda carried over the radio. Successive governments which have tried to use the radio as an instrument to promote their cause at a general election have failed in this endeavour. The general election of 1970, for instance, was preceded by a massive propaganda campaign over the radio aimed at convincing the people of the success of the government of the day in increasing food production. Yet the outcome of the general election showed that this campaign had had no influence on the result and had therefore failed to convince or to make enthusiastic the people, although in this case the major daily and weekly newspapers also participated in the campaign on the same side.

The conversion of Radio Ceylon into a broadcasting corporation has made no difference to the relations between the radio and the State. In effect, what took place in 1966 was merely a change of name and of the mechanics of organization, but in its mode of functioning, broadcasting policies and content of broadcasting matter, the Sri Lanka Broadcasting

Corporation has functioned throughout the last decade as the direct instrument of the government of the day. The hopes and expectations of the 1966 commission have not been borne out by the corporation's actual record.

The failure of the radio to meet the ends of national development has been as striking in the field of education. Successive commissions of inquiry have drawn attention to this failure. The commission of 1953 said:[1]

From the evidence before us, both oral and written, on the subject of Schools Broadcasting, one fact emerges very clearly, and that is the lack of co-ordination of the transmitting and receiving ends. In other words, there is a gap between Radio Ceylon and the schools in regard to planning at one end and listening-in at the other. There is no effective machinery in the Education Department to ensure that school broadcasts, planned and produced by Radio Ceylon, are actually listened to by schools, and that the Educational authorities co-operate with the Radio Ceylon staff to make School Broadcasting a success.

Twenty years later, these words continued to be true, as is confirmed by the comments of later commissions. The 1966 commission wrote:[2]

The School Broadcasting Service of Radio Ceylon was inaugurated in 1931, under the auspices of the Director of Education. 34 years later, persons holding responsible positions in the Department of Education and of Radio Ceylon, respectively, have said in their evidence before us that it is a waste of time. This is a sad confession of failure. We must surmise that, if the service was superfluous, it would have been discontinued many years ago as a costly experiment that had not produced significant results. Its survival cannot be due only to a victory of hope over experience: there has always been a nagging feeling among all concerned that, despite poor performance, Radio Ceylon had an obligation to make a contribution to formal education, as national systems of broadcasting are doing the world over.

By the time the commission of inquiry on the Ceylon Broadcasting Corporation in 1972 reported, this contribution was still being awaited. The majority report of the commission stated:[3]

Almost all the Regional Directors of Education and nearly everyone who gave evidence before us admitted that the Schools broadcasting service was not a success.

The minority report stated fully both the magnitude of the potentialities of the radio in education and the extent to which it had failed to measure up to these potentialities:[4]

1. *Report of the Commission on Broadcasting,* op. cit., Para. 278.
2. *Report of the Commission on Broadcasting and Information,* op. cit., Para. 154.
3. *Report of the Commission on the Ceylon Broadcasting Corporation,* Para. 224, Colombo, 1972.
4. *A Report on the Ceylon Broadcasting Corporation and Mass Media,* Paras. 236–8, Colombo, 1972.

The greatest service the Radio can render the community is in the field of education of the young. This is obvious and this is what everybody expects the Radio to do; particularly in a country where sufficient facilities for education are still lacking, and the people themselves are most interested in giving their children the best possible education.

But for forty years, for one reason or another, the Radio has not made much progress in this direction. The C.B.C. Education Service functions in a vacuum without any recognition by the Education Department. This hoodoo must be broken. It is a pity that the Radio cannot serve this great purpose now, when the radio is best equipped to perform it because of the popularity of transistor sets.

Sri Lanka has no television, and is not likely to in the immediately foreseeable future. From time to time there have been foreign offers of assistance in setting up a television project, even of an outright grant of the transmitting equipment. But the deterrent against accepting such offers has always been that it would commit the government to permitting the import of receiving sets; this cannot be contemplated at a time when foreign exchange is scarce even for essential foodstuffs.

Expenditure on the installation of television would be all the more indefensible at the present time since it would be a luxury of the rich. It might be argued that television could be a powerful educational aid, but here again beneficiaries of an educational television programme, transmitted from a station which would inevitably be sited in Colombo, would be the schools in the capital city and the immediately surrounding areas, which are already better equipped and better staffed than those in remoter provincial areas.

It is possible, however, that with the rapid development of television in India, linked to a satellite network, there will be a small group of television viewers in Sri Lanka who will pick up these foreign programmes on domestic receiving sets. There is little likelihood, however, of television becoming a national mass medium in the near future.

5 The film in Sri Lanka

The film industry in Sri Lanka originally grew up through the import and distribution of foreign films in the first decade of this century. The first public screening of films in the island is believed to have been in 1903 in a hall in Colombo. In succeeding years, a film company by the name of Madan Theatres which owned a chain of cinemas in India set up a number of cinemas in Colombo as well as in some provincial towns.

Enterprises of Sri Lanka began to enter the film industry in an effective way only in 1928, when the firm of Ceylon Theatres Ltd was founded by Chittampalam A. Gardiner (later Sir) and his associates. With the establishment and growth of this enterprise, the import, distribution and exhibition of films began to pass from the foreign interests that had controlled these fields to the hands of people of Sri Lanka. Ceylon Theatres Ltd grew into a powerful organization dominating the industry, and had virtually no competitors until the late 1940s.

During the silent-film era, films from many different parts of the world were imported into Sri Lanka and exhibited here, because the nature of the medium presented no barriers of language. With the coming of sound in the late 1920s, however, these barriers began to make themselves felt. The socially privileged minority who were educated in English found their entertainment in the American and also, in course of time, in the British cinema. The mass film-going public, however, for whom the Western cinema mirrored a sophisticated and remote world that was alien to them, turned to the Indian cinema, especially the products of the Madras and Bombay studios. The Tamil-language cinema of southern India found a ready-made audience in the indigenous Tamil-speaking population of Sri Lanka and in the sizeable group of Tamil-speaking persons of Indian origin, especially among plantation workers. However, even Sinhala-speaking audiences who were not culturally Westernized found themselves to some extent at home with the Tamillanguage or Hindi cinema. In their eyes these products of the Indian film industry presented people and places which, however glamorized and dream-like, were still closer to the world they knew than the images of the Western cinema. The Indian cinema also used a leisurely and semi-operatic form that had some similarity to the indigenous traditions of theatre with which local audiences were familiar. However, with the growth of national consciousness, the domination of the screen by foreign, principally

40

Indian films, was to create serious and controversial problems—problems that have in fact not been fully resolved even today.

As in all countries, the film industry in Sri Lanka in the early stages of its growth had to meet with a certain resistance from conservative sections of the public who regarded the cinema as an inferior and morally subversive medium. However, this resistance was gradually overcome, and by the latter part of the 1940s, the cinema had outstripped the theatre as the most popular form of mass entertainment; in fact, around this time, it pushed the indigenous Sinhala-language theatre into a state of near-extinction which lasted until the revival of stage drama in 1956 and after.

The growing popularity of the cinema was reflected in the formation of two new powerful companies which entered the field of film import and distribution—Ceylon Entertainments Ltd, founded in 1946, and Cinemas Ltd, formed in 1949. With the establishment of these two companies as competitors to the older and flourishing enterprise of Ceylon Theatres Ltd, the film industry became in effect a monopoly of three companies which controlled nearly the whole of film importation into Sri Lanka, and through their three circuits entirely dominated film distribution and exhibition, not only in the cinemas they owned but also in those owned by small exhibitors to whom they rented films. Moreover, this monopoly was soon strengthened by various agreements between these three companies to protect their joint interests. Speaking of these agreements, the Commission of Inquiry into the Film Industry in Ceylon said in its report in 1964:[1]

These agreements have necessarily restricted the possible area of competition between the three groups even while they have made it immensely more difficult for any other interests even to venture to compete with them. Such agreements are, of course, a natural development in any industry where economic power passes into the hands of a few groups.

Until 1947 the film industry in Sri Lanka existed only as a dependant of the international film industry since its activity was confined to the importation and screening of films made in other countries. There were a few sporadic attempts at film-making in the silent era, and one film, *Royal Adventure,* made in 1925 by A. G. Noorbhai, an exhibitor of films, was actually completed but was destroyed by fire during a screening abroad, and was never seen by audiences in Sri Lanka.

With the coming of sound and the growth of the film audience there was, by the 1940s, an opportunity for making indigenous feature films in the language of the majority of the people, Sinhala. However, the initiative for beginning film-making in Sri Lanka did not come from the big interests who then dominated the industry, because they were already doing well financially out of the import and exhibition of foreign films and therefore

---

1. *Report of the Commission of Inquiry on the Film Industry,* Para. 72, Colombo, 1964.

41

had no incentive to promote a national film industry. It was an independent producer, S. M. Nayagam, who made the first Sinhala film, *Kadavunu Poronduva (Broken Promise)* in 1947. However, the commercial success of his enterprise compelled Ceylon Theatres Ltd also to enter the field of film-making with the second Sinhala feature film, *Asokamala,* in the same year. Thus the national cinema was born.

At this stage, however, the Sinhala feature film could be described as 'national' only in a restricted sense—that it used local actors and artistes and that its dialogues and songs were in the Sinhala language. Since no studio facilities existed at that time for the making of films within the country, the early Sinhala films were shot entirely in studios in southern India, and consequently used southern Indian directors, technicians and musicians. Moreover, although the first two Sinhala films used the plot of a popular stage play and a legend from Sri Lanka history as their story material, many other film producers turned to the easier course of copying the plots, dialogue and songs of Indian films, and sometimes even their cinematic presentation, shot by shot. Thus the Sinhala film at this stage became, in the words of the film commission 'a servile imitation of a foreign product'.

The first attempt to break with the domination of the Indian film over the Sinhala screen was by an independent film-maker, Lester James Peries, who had worked in documentary cinema and was well acquainted with the traditions of Western cinema. His first feature film, *Rekava* (1956) was also the first Sinhala film to be shot entirely in Sri Lanka using real locations and employing technicians of Sri Lanka. But, the film was too sophisticated and too remote from the film idiom to which the mass audience was then accustomed to be a commercial success. However, in the next decade there gradually emerged a handful of films which sought to create a national idiom in cinema and to present indigenous life more faithfully by breaking away from the pattern set by the Madras and Bombay studios; and some of these films succeeded in making contact with a popular audience, sections of which were becoming more discriminating in their taste with the growth of education.

Meanwhile, the establishment of studios for film production in Sri Lanka eliminated the necessity for film-makers to travel to southern India to shoot their films. Here, again, the first initiative came not from the big monopoly groups but from a small independent producer, Sirisena Wimalaweera, who set up a modest studio in 1951. Later the big companies entered this field, Ceylon Theatres Ltd in 1956 and Cinemas Ltd in 1962. With the establishment of these studios the government imposed a ban on film-makers going outside the country to shoot Sinhala films.

In spite of the small progress made in the 1950s towards the growth of a truly national cinema, the fundamental problem of the industry was that of monopoly control. Hence in the years 1960–62, there was considerable agitation on the part of persons interested in the development of the national film industry—some film-makers and artistes, critics and journalists, cultural and social organizations, and certain members of Parliament—asking for State intervention to end the evils of monopoly in the film industry. The government responded to this agitation by appointing the Commission of Inquiry into the Film Industry in 1962. The terms of reference of the commission included among others: (a) the proper relationship between the producer and the distributor which would prevent the exploitation of the producer by the distributor; (b) the measures to be taken to improve the quality of films; (c) the establishment of a corporation to take over the import of films.

The commission in its report presented in 1964 held that the film industry in Sri Lanka was a monopoly in the sense that it was based on 'the concentration in a few hands of financial power (carrying with it all other forms of power) over the industry'. At the time there were five circuits, of which the three operated by the principal distributors controlled all but 13 of the 274 cinemas in the country. The breakdown of the cinemas was as follows: Ceylon Theatres Ltd, 108; Cinemas Ltd, 125; Ceylon Entertainments Ltd, 28; Odeon Cinemas, 5; Cinetones Ltd, 6; unattached, 2.

The three big groups also controlled the greater part of film imports; and through the studios that two of them owned, through the films they made themselves as well as through their financing of independent producers, they dominated film production within the country. Thus the monopolistic structure of the industry covered all its areas: import, distribution, production and exhibition.

The commission held that this monopolistic structure had led to the financial exploitation of both the independent producer and the small exhibitor by the distributor; that it had hampered the growth of the national cinema by the importer-distributors' preference for foreign (especially Indian) films as against the national product because they made larger profits out of the former; and that the monopoly groups had stood in the way of the creative growth of the Sinhala film because of their attachment to the film formulas of the Madras and Bombay studios on which their own taste had been nurtured.

As in the case of the press, the inevitable consequence of the abuse of monopoly power was State intervention. The film commission, in common with representatives of public opinion who appeared before it, took the view that 'there should be a measure of State intervention and control, though not a complete take-over of the industry':[1]

Accordingly our recommendations have been directed towards giving the State that degree of control and participation in the industry that is necessary for its healthy growth while preserving for producers, directors and artistes the freedom to engage in creative activity. We believe that this approach is best suited to the social, economic and political structure at present prevailing in Ceylon.

---

1. *Report of the Commission of Inquiry on the Film Industry,* op. cit., Para 286.

The commission therefore recommended the establishment of a National Film Corporation which would perform three functions: (a) to undertake the import and distribution of films; (b) to run a studio to provide facilities to local film producers; (c) to undertake the production of educational and cultural documentaries and children's films. Import and distribution of films would be taken entirely out of the hands of the private sector, though production and exhibition of films would remain open to private enterprise. The import of foreign films was to be restricted in order to protect and develop the national product; financial assistance by way of loans was to be given by the Corporation to film producers; and various measures were to be adopted to encourage the production of good-quality films.

In summing up its recommendations the Commission stated:[1]

Our recommendations . . . have been directed primarily towards breaking up the existing monopoly in the industry and of creating the conditions under which creative effort and activity could flourish freely so that the standards of the industry might be raised and the film might function as a healthy social and cultural medium. We do not believe that the problems of the film industry can be approached from a purely commercial or financial standpoint as if the film were no different from any commodity which is bought and sold on the market. Public policy in relation to the film industry has to be guided by an awareness of the far-reaching effect that the film has on society, on its culture and religion, its manners, morals and social outlook.

A change of government in 1965 almost immediately after the publication of the report led to its being shelved for five years. At the general election of 1970, however, the future of the film industry was one of the issues embodied in the election manifesto of the United Front which won the election. The new government proceeded to introduce a Bill for the establishment of a State Film Corporation, adopted in 1972. The corporation has since progressively entered and widened the area of its operation in the fields of import and distribution, until in 1976 it has taken over completely the import of foreign films as well as the distribution of all films, whether foreign or nationally produced. The corporation has begun a scheme for the grant of loans to film producers through a State-owned bank subject to the approval of scripts by the corporation, and it is preparing to establish its own studio to provide facilities for production. It also controls the issue of raw stock to film-makers.

Although the private monopoly in the film industry has been broken, the State Film Corporation faces its own problems. In the first few years of its operation, it has been concerned mainly with the mechanics of the takeover of import and distribution. With the completion of this process, it confronts the more complex and difficult question of its fundamental objectives in relation to the national film industry. On the one hand, the corporation is

1. Report of the Commission of Inquiry on the Film Industry, op. cit., Para. 289.

a business enterprise which has to be commercially viable and to make a profit. On the other hand, it cannot, in the words of the film commission, approach the problems of the film industry 'from a purely commercial or financial standpoint as if the film were no different from any commodity which is bought and sold on the market'. On the success with which the corporation achieves this reconciliation between over-all commercial profitability and the larger social and cultural objectives for which it was set up, will depend its future.

One of the crucial areas in which this problem presents itself is that of competition between the foreign and the national film. The greater part of total screen time on a national scale is still taken up by the Indian film, which retains its popularity with film-goers because of the long addiction of the audience to its plots, formulas, stars and songs, and because of the technical resources of the Indian film, in the form of colour and lavish sets, that cannot be matched by the indigenous film. Thus it often happens that an Indian film imported and distributed by the State Film Corporation has a damaging effect on the popularity and takings of a Sinhala film released at the same time—a repetition of the situation that existed in the time of the private distributors. Moreover, since that time the problems of the indigenous film producer have been accentuated by greatly increased costs of raw stock and production arrangements, and the most unfortunate feature of this situation is that these handicaps tell most heavily on the more serious-minded film-maker who is trying to improve the quality of films. In these circumstances, how far can the State Film Corporation go in making money out of imported films without hampering the national film? This will be one of the central issues to be decided in the near future.

So far this chapter has been concerned with the feature film which is regarded by the mass audience fundamentally as a medium of entertainment, but which, often invisibly, shapes the outlook and values of its audience and thus is an important medium of mass communication. There is, however, also another important aspect of cinema: the documentary, which is directly concerned with instructing, educating or persuading its audience. In Sri Lanka, documentary film-making as a regular activity dates from the establishment of the Government Film Unit shortly after independence—in 1949—as a section of the Department of Information. This unit (now renamed the Films Division of the Department of Information) still makes the greater part of the documentary films produced in Sri Lanka. The range of films produced by it includes news-reels as well as films publicizing the activities of the government in various economic and social fields, instructional and informational films directed towards agricultural, health or population education, and documentaries of a cultural character.

Outside the Films Division of the Department of Information, documentary films are also produced by private film-makers when commissioned by the government, a corporation or other public institution, or by a commercial enterprise for purposes of publicity and advertising. There have also been a few short documentary films made by individual film-makers as a creative activity. These may increase in number in the future since the State Film Corporation has begun a programme to encourage the production of such short films by fledgling film-makers.

Documentary films made by the Films Division of the Department of Information are screened not only in the cinemas but also in school halls, community centres and open-air sites by projector-equipped vans which take films to many parts of the country, particularly to rural areas unserved by cinemas.

If the parallel between the operation of the feature-film industry in Sri Lanka under a private monopoly and the press under a similar monopoly was very close, a similar parallel can be drawn between the State-owned radio and the State-owned Film Unit or Films Division. The film commission said in its report:[1]

This task of film-making is a creative one requiring initiative, imagination and enthusiasm. The Government Film Unit taken as a whole did not appear to us to have these qualities. Their attitude appeared to be no better than that of any department performing routine administrative functions.

However, while the radio has at least kept its programmes going week by week, the volume of documentary film production by the Films Division has been meagre, and the greater part of its budget, as the film commission pointed out, has been 'spent on salaries and overhead charges and only a small fraction on production'. Its most regular activity has been the production of a periodical news-reel which, under successive governments, has been the subject of criticism for its excessive concentration on political personalities and on opening ceremonies and other such functions in which these personalities participate. It has often been pointed out that the dullness of these news-reels and their obtrusion of individual personalities have been a handicap rather than a service to any government by provoking a negative reaction on the part of audiences. Although in recent years there has been a slight increase in the volume of documentary film-making as compared with news-reels, the Films Division has a long way to go before it can claim to have developed documentary cinema as a dynamic mass medium focusing attention on the whole range of the country's social, economic and cultural life.

1. *Report of the Commission of Inquiry on the Film Industry,* op. cit., Para. 254.

6 Communication professions in Sri Lanka

Professional associations of persons engaged in the mass media in Sri Lanka have never reached a high degree of organization. In the period before 1956, journalists and other persons employed in newspaper enterprises were prevented by their proprietors from forming or joining trade unions. Although these barriers disappeared in the new social and political climate after 1956, there has not grown up a trade union organization entirely devoted to the protection of the rights and interests of journalists, though many journalists as well as those working on the radio have joined trade unions which include broader sections of workers. There are, however, two associations of journalists, which are not trade unions but function more as professional clubs.

Film artistes and technicians are even less organized, because most of them do not work as permanent employees for any institution or enterprise but are hired temporarily for each film project, and this has made unionization of film artistes and technicians difficult. Though some associations of film actors and artistes were active in the agitation of 1960–62 which led to the setting up of the film commission and in the subsequent general election campaigns, their activity has been of a sporadic character.

Training facilities in the skills and functions of the mass media have also been very slow in developing in Sri Lanka. Most of the personnel engaged in the various mass media at present—whether in press, radio or film—have acquired whatever skills they possess on the job, and have not undergone any systematic or organized training. A small group of them have had opportunities for training in institutions in the Western countries. The quality of this training varies in character, and even where such training has been received in an institution of repute, it is not always relevant and applicable to conditions prevailing in Sri Lanka, where the technological and social contexts differ from those in Western countries.

In 1968, the Sri Lanka Broadcasting Corporation set up a training institute, which provided in-service training for producers, announcers, news reporters and other operational staff through seminars and workshops. Some training classes were also conducted for broadcasters outside the regular staff of the corporation: feature writers, drama personnel and script-writers.

A training course in film techniques has been conducted by the Films Division of the Department of Information during the last few years for a small group of young aspirants to careers in the film industry. The trainees are given an understanding of all the different skills involved in film-making through lectures, screening and study of films, as well as practical experience of participation in film-making. The course, however, is not tied directly to employment opportunities, though trainees may claim this experience as a qualification in applying for jobs in the Films Division of the Department of Information or in the private feature film sector.

In 1975 the State Film Corporation conducted a short-term seminar on film-script writing. The corporation has compiled a register of directors and other technicians recognized by the corporation. The basis for inclusion in this register is previous experience in film-making and the quality of work done is not taken into account as a criterion. In order to be included on the register of directors, for instance, it is necessary and sufficient to have already made at least one feature film. Applications for financial loans for film projects and for the issue of raw stock for them are approved by the corporation only where the persons involved in these projects have been registered as film-makers with previous film experience. Others may gain registration by passing a test conducted by the corporation and by making a short film, with the help of facilities provided by the corporation.

Until recently there were no opportunities for the study of mass media in any educational institution in Sri Lanka. In 1969, the junior university colleges set up by the government of the day provided a course in journalism and mass communications. However, with a change of government in 1970, the junior university colleges were themselves wound up. In 1972, the Faculty of Humanities of the Colombo Campus of the University of Sri Lanka included 'elements of journalism' in its course of studies for the B.Phil. degree. Following this, the Vidyalankara Campus of the university established a Department of Mass Communications, and made mass communications a subject that students could offer for their B.A. degree. The main drawback to these studies is their exclusively academic character, the absence of a relationship between these university studies and the day-to-day activity of the mass media themselves, and the lack of definite employment opportunities for those who complete these courses. In these circumstances, it is possible for a student who has gained a theoretical knowledge of the mass media either to be unemployed or to find employment in some altogether different career, in which case his study of the mass media would have been wasted.

There has been no organized attempt to build up a code of ethics for journalists and other persons engaged in the mass media, although criticism of journalistic behaviour has been frequently made from political platforms, in the evidence of witnesses before the press commission, and by the press commission itself in its report. As has already been mentioned, one of the functions assigned to the Press Council when it was set up in 1973 was 'to ensure on the part of newspapers and journalists the maintenance of high standards of journalistic ethics, and to foster a due sense of both the rights and responsibilities of citizenship'. The Press Council, however, has so far not concerned itself with this function, except to the extent that journalistic and newspaper ethics become an issue in its inquiries into specific complaints made against a news item or article. It may be argued that the very existence of the Press Council and its powers to order corrections and apologies or to censure publishers, editors and journalists is a deterrent to unethical behaviour. This has some truth only in so far as it pertains to the publication of material unfairly damaging to the reputation of an individual or detrimental to an organization. However, unethical practices in newspapers are not confined to material of this kind. Equally important is the need to prevent the columns of newspapers being used unjustifiably to boost or promote individuals and organizations. It has often been observed that there are journalists who act as public relations men for persons in positions of importance and use the columns of the newspapers to advance their interests. This kind of activity is not likely to be the subject of inquiry by the Press Council in its present mode of functioning, since in practice the only unethical practices that are likely to be brought before it are defamatory or damaging material complained of by aggrieved persons. It must finally be remarked that there is no regulation of unethical practices in radio, even to the limited extent that the Press Council provides a curb on such practices in relation to newspapers, although the Commission of Inquiry on the Ceylon Broadcasting Corporation in 1972 commented strongly on the misuse of the radio on the eve of the general election of 1970 in an attempt to involve one of the highest ranking Buddhist prelates in controversial and partisan election politics.

7 Social participation in communication

The main organization responsible for disseminating and publicizing news and information on behalf of the government is the Department of Information, set up under the Ministry of Information and Broadcasting. It maintains liaison with and feeds information to the various mass media—press, radio and cinema—on behalf of the government. Each ministry has attached to it press officers who belong to the personnel of the Department of Information, and who brief mass media about the policies and activities of ministries and government departments.

The Department of Information also puts out periodically news-sheets, booklets, pamphlets and posters to publicize the government's policies and projects.

The head of the Department of Information is the Director of Information. The Films Division also comes within his purview.

In recent times however the government has not relied solely on the mass media and the co-ordinating activity of the Department of Information to make known whatever messages it wishes to communicate to the people in various spheres of activity. In various fields, such as agriculture, health and rural development, there is a large number of extension workers functioning at the grass roots level to carry to the people knowledge of new techniques of farming, use of fertilizers, high-yielding varieties of paddy, sanitation practices, methods of controlling epidemics, and the like. In the field of rural development, locally based rural-development officers help to harness voluntary effort for purposes such as the building of roads, reconstruction of tanks, and starting of small industries.

All this activity is carried on mainly through direct interpersonal communication at the level of the small village community. The success of much of this activity is a proof of what has been said in the opening chapters about the importance of this form of communication as an agency of development. If the Department of Agriculture or the Department of Health relied solely on the mass media to convey the essential information they wanted to communicate and to enlist popular participation in their programmes, they would fail. Even though Sri Lanka has a largely literate population, the mass media by themselves cannot evoke enthusiasm and active response to a new idea or project. On the contrary, in isolation they would be likely to meet with scepticism and even with resistance. It is necessary to overcome these reactions by personal contact at the local level, by engaging in dialogue with the people, by meeting objections and doubts patiently and understandingly. The same message that may appear cold and remote when carried by a newspaper or over the radio takes on more life and meaning when brought to the village by the familiar figure of the Agricultural Extension Officer or the Rural Development Officer, who communicates personally with the people.

A detailed examination follows of one experiment in promoting a population education project using various modes of communication. This was a pilot project for the distribution of condoms in Sri Lanka, undertaken in 1973 by the International Planned Parenthood Federation (IPPF). The IPPF (Indian Ocean region) organ, *Future,* describes as follows the problems that confronted the organization in undertaking this programme in Sri Lanka:[1]

In October 1973 IPPF launched a pilot project for the distribution of condoms in a community that was highly conservative in its attitude towards the free sale of condoms. They were available only in a few of the bigger chemists' shops in the urban areas; even the more sophisticated among them served their customers surreptitiously—not because it was illegal but because social disapproval was strong. It was the practice in a leading department store to assume that the few customers it had for condoms would purchase them for cash rather than have the transaction recorded in their credit accounts. The word 'condom' was not used in polite society. Public advertising was unthinkable. Even today the word may not be used over the State controlled radio.

In spite of these problems, the project was so successful that within seven months of its being launched, 2 million condoms were sold. 'Even the most enthusiastic supporters of the project', comments *Future,* 'could not have expected such quick success.'

How was this success made possible, and how were the barriers of conservatism, prejudice and ignorance overcome? The promotion programme for the condom, which was sold under the name 'Preethi' (Joy) included large-scale advertising in the press. But what was crucial to the success of the project was that it was decided to make the condom available not just in chemists' shops but throughout the country through the network of small tradesmen's shops from which people in town and village obtained their daily necessities such as soap or salt. To draw the proprietors of these shops into the campaign involved a task of direct interpersonal communication and persuasion, thus described by *Future:*

In a small rural community the nexus between the small shopkeeper and the community is not always a purely impersonal business relationship. The local shopkeeper is often a well-known figure in the village. If he has been fairly successful, he begins to play the role of philanthropist, contributing to the building of community centres, schools and towards the expenses of local festivals and functions. The initial reaction of such a person to the handling of a disreputable product was

1. IPPF (Indian Ocean region), *Future,* November-December 1975.

naturally not a very enthusiastic one. One of the first tasks was to make him understand the rationale of family planning and make him feel that he was an extension worker in a social cause rather than simply a vendor of condoms for profit. This did not mean that he was not to be provided with a profit margin; but profit alone would not have induced many of his kind in the beginning to handle the product.

Even the more sophisticated and educated people employed in the metropolis for packing 'Preethi' were reluctant to handle it, but changed their attitude after a seminar specially organised for them in which the subject of family planning was discussed in its broad perspectives.

In one area of the island, a field educator of the project was also employed to speak to groups of men and women and thus popularize the use of the condom by direct person-to-person motivation. *Future* says, describing his talks: 'By stretching and releasing a condom in his hands, while talking about 'Preethi', he helps to get rid of the shyness associated with contraceptives.'

The results of the IPPF project in an area of activity where many obstacles had to be overcome in communicating a message to the people can be taken as a general model for promoting ideas for national development. Of course, 'Preethi' would not have become popular if it had not fulfilled a real need of the people. But even though the need existed, it was still necessary to convince the people of the answer, to overcome inhibitions and doubts, to evoke support and participation. The role of interpersonal communication at the local level is decisive in achieving these objectives in many spheres of national development.

8 Conclusions and trends

It will be apparent from the survey that has been made in the preceding chapters that communication policies have gone through three periods of evolution in Sri Lanka. In the period before 1956 the mass media were dominated by uncontrolled and unregulated private enterprise. The exception was the radio, which was from its beginning in colonial times a monopoly of the State. This was due, however, not to any considered policy on the part of the State. As has been mentioned earlier, the official committee which originally reported on the establishment of broadcasting in Sri Lanka recommended that it should be thrown open to private enterprise. That it was inaugurated under the auspices of the State was a largely fortuitous development.

Towards the press and the film the policy of the State before independence was one of *laissez-faire*. This policy was continued by governments even after independence until 1956, because the interests that dominated these mass media at the time were allied to those who held governmental power. Meanwhile, both the press and the cinema developed into private monopolies which enjoyed unrestrained power.

The abuse of this power by the private monopolies in press and cinema led to the realization by governments, in the changed social and political climate after 1956, that the policy of *laissez-faire* was inadequate in their own interests as well as in the general interests of society. The period between 1956 and 1970 was occupied by much thinking and discussion on this subject. The active concern of governments during this period with the need to end private monopoly power in the mass media is reflected in various public pronouncements and by the appointment of two commissions—the film commission of 1962 and the press commission of 1964. However, the correlation of political forces during this period did not permit governments to pass from concern with the problem of monopoly to practical action.

This came in the 1970s through both statutory and administrative action. This period has been characterized by the increasing State intervention in the mass media in order to regulate indiscriminate use of mass media for private needs. The conversion of the Associated Newspapers of Ceylon Ltd into a public corporation, the closure of the Independent Newspapers Ltd, the creation of the Press Council and the establishment of the State Film Corporation to take over the import and distribution of films, have to a large extent ended the private monopoly over the mass media. It is, however, left to the Press Council and to the other controlling bodies connected with the other mass media organizations to implement government objectives in bringing about a drastic change in the ownership of the mass media.

It can be expected that in the years to come society in Sri Lanka will be concerned with the problems resulting from this changed balance of forces in the field of the mass media. It can be stated categorically that under no circumstances is there likely to be a return to the old policy of *laissez-faire*. There will always be a need for State intervention in and regulation of the mass media in the public interest. But it can be predicted that Sri Lanka will have to discover by experience the right balance between such intervention and regulation and the fundamental need to preserve freedom of expression and ensure the people's continuing right to choose freely between a variety of contending opinions.

It is certain that Sri Lanka will continue to evolve in the direction of an egalitarian society based on democratic forms of government. Whatever the social and economic structures her people choose, mixed economy or completely collectivist and co-operative forms of ownership, there can be no doubt that they will not wish to abandon the democratic rights of freedom of expression and of access to the widest possible range of opinions and views.

Certain writers on the mass media, particularly in Western countries, have portrayed the people as a captive audience who can be moulded and manipulated by the mass media in any direction that those who operate these media may choose. The experience of Sri Lanka, as set out in this study, shows that in this country at least this conception of the mass audience is a false one. The public in Sri Lanka has shown itself to be far from passive in relation to the mass media; on the contrary it has proved to be alert, critical and independent in its judgements, with a healthy scepticism towards the mass media and a capacity to take or reject what is offered by the media depending on its acceptability or otherwise on the basis of their own experience and knowledge of the truth. The continuing active tradition of oral and interpersonal communication has given the mass audience in Sri Lanka an independent standard from which to judge the contents of the mass media and an alternative mode of expression and communication which prevent them from becoming defenceless before the media.

It can be stated that no communication policy on the part of those who control the media, whether private interests or State organizations, will be successful unless it takes account of this capacity of the people for independent judgement. Over and over again in the recent history of Sri Lanka those who believed that the people were merely raw material to be manipulated as those who controlled the mass media desire have come to grief.

A variety of contending opinions is therefore necessary in the interests of not only the people but also the State. It must be remarked that whenever press and radio have projected only an uncritically favourable image of the activities and achievements of any government, they have done a disservice to the very cause they were seeking to promote. The mass media have a good deal to do with the several changes of government in the last twenty years, since many voters have been impelled at a general election to reject a ruling administration by the extravagant claims made on its behalf by the mass media and the gulf between the projected image and the reality.

What organizational forms will emerge in course of time to maintain the balance between State intervention in the public interest and freedom of expression cannot be predicted at this stage; but in the interests of democracy and the freedom of the people it behoves the government to exercise great care and caution in the use of the mass media.

Appendix:
Statistical data on Sri Lanka

The island of Sri Lanka lies twenty-two miles from the nearest point of southern India, 400 miles north of the Equator.

Sri Lanka has an area of 25,332 square miles—270 miles long and 140 miles wide at the widest point.

The population in 1971 was 12.7 million (12,747,755—1971 census). Of the population 52 per cent are males and 48 per cent are females.

Annual rate of growth is 2.3 per cent.

Racially the population is divided between: Sinhalese, 70 per cent; Tamils, 22 per cent (Sri Lanka Tamils, 11 per cent; Indian Tamils 11 per cent); Moors, 6 per cent; others, 2 per cent (Burghers, Eurasians, Malays, etc.).

By religion Buddhists form the great majority (66 per cent). The balance consist of Hindus (18 per cent), Christians (9 per cent), Muslims (7 per cent).

Sinhala, the language of the majority, is the official language and the medium of instruction in schools and universities, but due chiefly to a century and a half of British rule, English is widely spoken and understood. Tamil is spoken by the Tamils.

The rate of literacy is quite high. Leaving out children below 5 years, literacy has reached 78 per cent. Of the population 24 per cent have had at least a secondary education.

Of the population 80 per cent live in rural areas, only 20 per cent in urban areas; 40 per cent are under 14 years and 55 per cent are under 21 years.

TABLE 1. Population of Sri Lanka, 1921–71

Year	Population	Year	Population
1921	4,498,605	1963	10,582,064
1946	6,655,339	1971	12,711,143
1953	8,097,895		

TABLE 2. Statistics on education

Year	Schools	Teachers	Pupils	Graduates
1948	6,391	33,517	1,190,951	210
1958	7,880	62,689	2,013,147	528
1968	9,539	91,020	2,604,910	4,014
1973/74	8,945[1]	98,691	2,596,588[1]	3,673

1. Compulsory education age was changed from 5 years to 6 years with effect from 1972.

TABLE 3. Newspaper circulation

Language of newspaper	1968	1974
Sinhala dailies (7)	320,098	257,657
Tamil dailies (4)	63,297	54,971
English dailies (5)	121,447	129,324

TABLE 4. Radio licences

Year	Number	Year	Number
1948	30,000[1]	1968	280,581
1958	229,498	1974	455,368

1. The figure for 1948 is approximate.
Note: It is generally assumed that there are additionally at least half as many unlicensed radio sets in the country.

The number of locally produced films released in the country was as follows: 1948, 3; 1958, 9; 1968, 20; 1974, 22. The total number of cinemas in 1974 was 362 with a daily average of tickets issued, for 1973, of 139,136 and for 1974, 151,451.

TABLE 5. Books published in Sri Lanka

Language	1968		1974	
	Titles	Copies	Titles	Copies
Sinhala	872	4,505,058	557	4,750,977
Tamil	254	1,232,358	269	1,156,242
English	280	1,379,958	361	1,509,393
Pali	2	5,500	—	—
Sanskrit	3	4,081	1	1,000
Bilingual or multilingual	159	251,436	254	877,467
TOTAL	1,570	7,376,391	1,442	8,295,079